Ten Commandments

of

Financial Awareness

for

God's People

By Marcella "MJ" Haskins
B.B.A., C.P.F.C.

Library of Congress: 2024923295

ISBN: 9 780983 799627

Ten Commandments of Financial Awareness for God's People

2nd Edition

By Marcella "MJ" Haskins, B.B.A., C.P.F.C.

DEDICATION

First and foremost, I would like to dedicate this book to my Heavenly Father, Jesus the Christ. All knowledge and wisdom flow from You and I give you all the glory! I thank you for depositing in me all of my gifts, talents, and abilities, knowledge, wisdom and understanding. "But you are to remember the Lord your God, for it is He who is giving you power to make wealth, in order to confirm His covenant which, He swore to your fathers, as it is this day."

~ Deuteronomy 8:18

I would like to dedicate this book to the woman who taught me everything, most importantly, making lemonade out of lemons. I remember when we had no food in the kitchen except for flour and a bag of onions – you made my sister and I onion rings to feed us. That was brilliant! I admire you for your strength and resilience. I was born with a disability but never thought I was disabled because you never allowed me to pity myself and encouraged me to push through. You wrapped me in your love, instruction, and correction. You gave me peace and security. Thank you greatly for teaching me to read EVERYTHING. That lesson alone has borne much fruit in my life. Many more of your lessons have shaped my life including how to cook. Oh, how I miss coming home or waking up to the smell of a home cooked meal, seasoned with love. Continue to rest in Jesus, Mommy Dearest. All my love eternally, Marcella.

Honorable mentions:

Aunt Joanne Parker-Henry. Because I was named after her (Joanne), I can use the initials MJ in business and people never forget my name! Aunt Joanne, thank you for taking me along with you to work, seminars, field trips and college tours. Being with you exposed me to different lifestyles. I was so proud when my aunt pulled up in her Corvette or Lexus. You gave me something to aspire to be, also you opened the door for me to get a four-year degree. My forever gratitude and love...

Malaika Livingston, my sister. My older and only sister. You may not know that you had a great impact on my life because of your intelligence. You and mom were avid book readers and could read a book in two or three days. I still cannot do that until this day. Thank you for protecting me when you were left exposed, thank you for being brave for me when I did not have courage, and although we do not talk much, I thank you for always being there for me when I need you. Bluebirds.

Table of Contents

INTRODUCTION

I am pleased to introduce "The Ten Commandments of Financial Awareness for God's People," a book crafted to offer invaluable guidance to individuals on a subject that invariably impacts every one of us at some point in our lives – Financial Literacy. Financial literacy is an issue of paramount importance, yet it has regrettably received inadequate attention in America over the years.

Interestingly, in the early 1900s, financial education was an integral part of school curricula, alongside academic subjects like Mathematics and English. I ardently advocate for a return to this practice, reinstating financial education as an essential component of our children's learning.

My journey into the world of finances was marked by a conspicuous absence of financial education during my upbringing. I do not remember being exposed to essential money management principles. Consequently, I made significant financial blunders, unable to apply any acquired financial knowledge effectively.

Even during my college years as a business major, I was surprised to discover that financial education remained conspicuously absent from the curriculum. It was through a process of trial and error that I began to unravel the mysteries of

1

money. The realization soon dawned upon me that without a sound financial footing, I would be unable to meet my needs and desires. Furthermore, the importance of maintaining a good credit history became abundantly clear, as it determined my eligibility for loans and other financial products.

This new understanding reinforced my belief in the critical need for financial education. It was during my time in college, particularly in my Entrepreneurship class, that I experienced a profound awakening concerning money matters. Inspired by this awakening, I created a sample business plan, envisioning a venture dedicated to providing financial guidance. My goal was to assist individuals who had suffered setbacks in their credit histories and felt overwhelmed by the prospect of reclaiming financial stability.

Additionally, I aspired to impart the knowledge necessary for people to make informed investment decisions. This passion for empowering individuals to regain their rightful financial standing continued to burn brightly beyond my college years.

In writing this book, my primary objective was to create a resource on personal finances that would be easily comprehensible to all readers. You will find no convoluted jargon or intricate charts within these pages. Instead, I have strived to present clear, concise, and straightforward information that will serve as your compass, pointing you in the right direction as you embark on your journey toward financial awareness.

What is Financial Literacy?

Financial literacy is the cornerstone of sound financial decision-making and achieving economic well-being. It encompasses an individual's grasp of personal finance concepts and their capacity to apply this knowledge to enhance their financial situation. With a strong foundation in financial literacy, individuals may be able to manage their finances effectively and achieve long-term objectives like homeownership or retirement.

People with low levels of financial literacy often need help with basic money management tasks. They may need help to create and adhere to budgets, make informed investment choices, or understand the implications of taking on debt. Consequently, they may face financial instability, accumulate debt, and be ill-prepared for emergencies or life events.

Enhancing financial literacy is the initial and critical step toward bolstering economic well-being. It involves acquiring knowledge about fundamental financial principles, such as budgeting, saving, investing, and debt management. With improved financial literacy, individuals can make informed choices regarding their financial resources, effectively plan for their future, and secure financial independence.

Financial literacy equips individuals with

the skills to navigate complex economic systems, make prudent financial decisions, and set achievable financial goals. It empowers them to build a secure financial future, whether purchasing a home, saving for their children's education, or enjoying a comfortable retirement.

In summary, financial literacy is the foundation upon which economic stability and prosperity are built. It empowers individuals to take control of their finances, make informed choices, and work towards achieving their financial aspirations. By investing in financial education and continuously improving their financial literacy, individuals can pave the way for a more secure and prosperous future.

Financial Literacy Statistics

- Bankruptcy filings experienced a 13 percent increase in total, with business bankruptcies seeing a substantial surge of nearly 30 percent over the twelve-month period ending on September 30, 2023 (United States Court, 2023).

- According to a recent Morning Consult poll, approximately 10% of U.S. adults are categorized as "unbanked" because they lack a savings or checking account at a bank or credit union. Within this group, half of them, which accounts for 5% of all adults, reported that no one in their household possesses a bank account (U. S. News and World Report, 2022).

- In July 2023, 61% of adults were living paycheck to paycheck, marking a two-point increase compared to the previous year (Lending Club, 2022).

- Nearly 40% of American adults now report struggling to meet their monthly expenses, reflecting an increase from 34.4% in 2022 and 26.7% in 2021 (The State Science & Technology Institute (SSTI; 2023).

The following data come from Capital One

- American consumers currently maintain 564.5 million active credit card accounts, which equates to an average of 2 accounts for every American adult.

- On average, U.S. cardholders carry three credit cards and engage in 210 credit card transactions annually.

(Capitol One, 2023)

Key Categories of Financial Literacy for Individuals

Financial literacy for individuals encompasses several significant categories to ensure a well-rounded understanding of personal finance. These categories include:

- **Budgeting**: Understanding how to create and manage a budget, tracking income and expenses, and setting financial goals.

- **Saving and Investing**: Knowledge of different savings and investment options, such as savings accounts, stocks, bonds, mutual funds, and retirement accounts (e.g., 401(k)s and IRAs).

- **Debt Management**: Learning about various types of debt (e.g., credit card debt, student loans, mortgages) and strategies to manage and reduce it effectively.

- **Financial Planning**: Developing a comprehensive financial plan considering short-term and long-term goals, including retirement planning, education savings, and emergency funds.

- **Banking and Financial Institutions**: Understanding how banks and credit unions operate, including managing accounts, using banking services and evaluating financial products.

- **Credit Management**: Knowledge of credit reports, scores, and responsible credit card usage to maintain good credit health.

- **Insurance**: Understanding the basics of different types of insurance (e.g., health, auto, home) and how insurance works to protect against financial risks.

- **Taxes**: Familiarity with tax laws, deductions, credits, and how to file tax returns accurately.

- **Financial Decision-Making**: Developing critical thinking skills to make informed decisions about loans, investments, and significant financial choices.

- **Consumer Rights and Responsibilities**: Awareness of consumer rights, fraud prevention, and responsible financial behavior.

- **Retirement Planning**: Preparing for a secure retirement by learning about retirement account options, Social Security, and retirement income strategies.

- **Estate Planning**: Understanding the basics of wills, trusts, and other estate planning tools to protect and transfer assets to heirs.

- **Financial Well-Being**: Fostering a healthy mindset and money-related behaviors, including financial goal setting, stress management, and adapting to life changes.

These financial literacy categories cover a broad spectrum of financial knowledge. It is important to learn and understand the meanings of these financial categories and other personal financial terms. As you continue to grow in understanding and familiarity with these terms you can then strive to apply them to your financial lives. Strategic application will lead to informed decisions and better decisions will ultimately result in financial stability and security.

Factors Contributing to Declining Financial Literacy

Improving financial literacy is essential for community building, economic stability, and individual empowerment. It is not a choice. There has never been a greater important need to raise financial literacy given the ever-complex financial world. It is an essential ability that can change people's lives by empowering them to make wise decisions, safeguard their futures, and support the development of a society that is more financially robust.

A reduction in financial literacy and people's economic well-being has been caused by changes in personal financial dynamics, demographic trends, and increased consumer responsibility. Moreover, the existence of dubious lending practices has made these issues worse, highlighting the urgent need for better financial protection and education. Changes in personal financial dynamics, changing demographic patterns, and the increasing weight of consumer responsibility have all contributed to the degradation of financial literacy and the reduction in people's economic well-being.

These issues have been made worse by the spread of questionable lending practices, which emphasize the critical need for comprehensive financial education and protection programs. These programs are necessary to provide people with the knowledge and abilities they need to secure their financial futures and navigate the ever- complex financial landscape.

According to Lusardi & Messey (2023), modifications to the pension scheme and the growing complexity of financial products demand higher levels of expertise to handle.

Also, increased risks and inflation have an impact on people's financial security and well- being. Lusardi & Messey posits that in an economic crisis, a large number of individuals may be impacted by serious financial problems, which only affect a tiny percentage of the population. This team offers that people under 40 have lower average financial capability than people above 40. Further, according to Lusardi & Messey, reduced financial stability, poor financial practices, and inadequate financial literacy are all strongly correlated with financial stress and anxiety. People living in low-income households frequently do not have access to financial services, adequate consumer protection, or K–12 financial education that is taught in schools (Lusardi & Messey, 2023).

According to Urban and Valdes (2022), there has been a decline in financial literacy due to a rise in the number of wrong replies selected by respondents and an increase in the selection of "don't know" as a response choice. It is also important to note, according to this study team, that financial literacy has been declining over the previous ten years, despite its relevance.

Financial literacy is declining in all demographic categories, although it is declining more in younger persons (ages 18 to 39), women, and Black/African American respondents than in older, male, and white respondents (Urban & Valdes, 2022).

Benefits of Financial Literacy Training

Financial literacy encompasses the capacity to make well-informed and judicious financial choices, yielding numerous advantages. These include the realization of financial objectives, proficient money and debt management, cost reduction, prevention of financial losses, and the mitigation of credit risks. It empowers individuals to navigate their financial journeys adeptly, ensuring that their fiscal goals are met, resources are managed prudently, and potential pitfalls are averted. Financial literacy is a cornerstone for sound financial well-being, equipping individuals with the knowledge and skills needed to attain economic stability and secure their financial futures.

According to Weiss (2022), financial literacy alone is not the end. Just knowing financial literacy will lead to failure. With only 57% of adults in the United States considered financially literate, addressing this issue becomes imperative. Enhancing the financial literacy of the entire population is a commendable objective. However, numerous uncertainties persist regarding the most effective means to achieve it. Also, per Weiss, one thing is certain - American households lose more than $350 billion annually as a result of their lack of personal financial literacy. Making better financial decisions requires financial knowledge, but financial literacy on its own will not cut it since it is just one element of a much larger jigsaw that includes money, life, and psychology (Weiss, 2022).

NOTE TO READER:

Over the following ten chapters, you will be educated from a secular perspective, but I will also insert nuggets of wisdom from the Bible Scripture that frame each chapter. It has been my experience that some churches have neglected to address and educate God's People about personal finances.

In many cases, we see that the Pastor and some in leadership are financially stable and adept, but many of the laymen, some leaders, and the congregation are still struggling. Members are having difficulty making ends meet and are living from paycheck to paycheck. God says that He came to give us life abundantly. The Bible says the sinner's wealth is laid up for the righteous, but it seems as though some of the righteous are living in lack and poverty. This ought not be, especially when God owns all the riches of the world.

Are we seeking first the kingdom of God and His righteousness? God said He would supply all our needs. It is time that the Church of God's People addressed this topic because the Bible has a lot to say about money, starting with the fact that it is necessary and answers all things in this world.

Although we live in this world but are not of this world, we still need money. Not having

16

money or good credit makes it extremely difficult to function in this society. We cannot get around this reality and because of this reality, we must deal with our financial issues. It is time to heal our finances. When our finances are not healed, and out of order, it is hard for us to concentrate on our purpose, families, assignments, gifts, talents, and abilities that we are to use to evangelize and edify the church.

Unhealed finances cause major worries and stress in families, from the parents to the children. Many of us in church are bound, and in bondage because our finances restrict us from living our best lives in Christ Jesus.

In 2018, a well-known financial guru, Dave Ramsey, of Ramsey Solutions, performed a study citing that money is ruining marriages. The number one issue couples fight about is also a topic many couples avoid discussing - money. According to a new survey by Ramsey Solutions, money fights are the second leading cause of divorce, behind infidelity.

Statistics & Key Findings from the Survey: As given by Ramsey Solutions (n.d.) a significant portion, about 66% of marriages begin with financial obligations. Among those marriages that have lasted over a quarter of a century, 43% had initial debts, compared to 86% of marriages that have been ongoing for five years or fewer.

This latter group has double the incidence of starting out with debt than those in longer marriages.

Sixty-three percent of those with $50,000 or more in debt feel anxious about talking about their personal finances. Nearly half of the individuals surveyed (47%) who have consumer debt report that their debt levels cause them stress and anxiety (Ramsey, n.d.). The articles that I read noted, "When a husband and wife can eliminate debt, a shift happens in their marriage. There's a peace of mind they haven't experienced before," said Rachel Cruz, #1 New York Times best-selling author and personal finance reporter."

My Prayer and hope for God's people is to be free. Free in their mind, body, and soul, and especially in their finances.

~MJ Haskins

The Ten Commandments of
Financial Awareness for
God's People begin next.

Commandment 1
Create a Spending Plan

"The master was full of praise. Well done, my good and faithful servant. You have been faithful in handling this small amount, so now I will give you many more responsibilities. Let's celebrate together!" ~Matthew 25:21

Creating a spending plan and a budget is essential for achieving financial stability and meeting your financial goals. Without a well-structured plan, it is easy to overspend, accumulate debt, and struggle with financial stress. A spending plan helps you track your income, allocate funds for necessities, savings, and discretionary spending, and avoid impulsive purchases. The plan empowers you to make informed financial decisions, save for the future, and ensure your money aligns with your priorities and goals. In short, a spending plan is crucial for achieving financial security and peace of mind.

The word "spend" can be used in various contexts related to income and financial activities. **Spending Money**: This is the most common use of "spend." It refers to using your income to pay for goods and services, such as groceries, rent, utilities, entertainment, and other expenses.

Now that you understand why it is important to have a Spending Plan and how it can help you let us define what a Spending Plan is.

What is a Spending Plan? A spending plan is exactly what it sounds like. It is a plan for spending your income or money. A Spending Plan also goes by the name "Budget." I believe that most people misunderstand the meaning of budget by thinking that the intent or purpose of a budget is to restrict their spending or lifestyle, so I prefer to use the words "Spending Plan." A Spending Plan gives you all the control over your money; it is within your power how you spend what God has entrusted you.

Some people spend their money on frivolous things and neglect their major household responsibilities. Others, as the scripture above implies, are faithful (or responsible) over the little that Father God gives them. Once they show that they can be responsible over the little, God gives them more; when they are responsible over that, God then gives them much more, and they are responsible over that until their household is filled with plenty and that residence is overflowing with divine riches and wealth!

A Spending Plan shows you three main pieces of information about your monthly household finances:

1. Your Income

2. Your Expenses (Fixed & Variable)

3. Your Discretionary Income/Deficit

Income is funds you have coming into your household, typically within a month's time. Many people consider their main source of income, such as wages from a job, their only source of income, but there are many more types of income. Other types of income include government benefits or assistance, such as Social Security income, small business or gig income, unemployment checks, rental income, tax refunds, pensions, dividends or proceeds from stock, grants, or inheritances.

Expenses are money that you have going out of your household. There are two types of expenses: 1. Fixed Expenses and 2. Variable Expenses. Fixed expenses are bills that do not change from month to month, such as your mortgage or rent, automobile note, auto and life insurance payments, installment loan, streaming service (Netflix), property taxes, or mobile phone. Variable expenses are bills that may vary such as an electric & water bill (based on usage), groceries, entertainment, gas, clothing, auto repair, or takeout food.

When calculating the bills or expenses that will need to be paid each month, we tend only to consider our major bills such as mortgage/rent, phone, electric, water, and cable bills. There are dozens of variable expenses that go unrecognized, which is why it is so important to have or find a budget (spending plan) document or online money management application with a thorough list of fixed expenses. If you do not have your spending plan written on paper or outlined within an application, you will continue to be baffled by why you come up short every month (a deficit).

It is imperative that you have your spending plan on paper or track your spending by collecting receipts to see what you are truly spending your money on. A good suggestion is to track your spending for one month, and that tracking will give you an idea of the amount of money you spend on variable expenses each month.

Discretionary Income or Deficit

The last piece of a Spending Plan I will present is your Discretionary Income or Deficit. Discretionary Income is defined as money that is left over after all your household expenses have been paid or a Deficit occurs when your expenses exceed your income. In plain language, Discretionary Income means you will have monthly income left over to spend on anything you want, such as investments, vacations, hobbies, etc. In simple terms, a Deficit means not only do you not have monthly income left, but you have overextended your financial capacity by living above your means. This also typically means that you are surviving off credit cards to help pay your household bills, borrowing money from friends and family, or simply not able to pay all your household bills and expenses.

As a Financial Coach-Consultant, many of my clients do not have Discretionary Income. About 65% of my clients have a Deficit, but this action can be reconciled. One way to reconcile a deficit is to get a second job or side gig to bring in additional income, go back to college, or get a specialized certification to increase your pay or get a promotion at your job. You can also reduce your spending in the categories where you feel you are spending too much money.

As believers two expenses that should be mandatory and included in your spending plan are Tithes/Offerings/Donations and Savings. We know that when we give God the first fruits of our income, God will cover the rest.

There is no tithe in the New Testament under the New Covenant. The Bible says, "Whatever you give is acceptable if you give it eagerly. And give according to what you have, not what you do not have." This means if you make $3000 each month, your monthly giving should be at least something reasonable such as 10% which is $300 per month, but don't stop there! If your heart is willing you can give 20, 30, or 40% of your monthly income up to 100%. Yes, I said up to 100% because you cannot out give God! Now this scripture works the same way if you are making $3000 each month, but your monthly expenses and commitments only allow you to give 5% each month or $20 each month. The Bible declares that if you give cheerfully, in proportion to what you can afford, and on a consistent basis (every pay period), you will be honoring this scriptural commandment.

One final thing that I want to mention is the Household Bills Hierarchy. This phrase means paying your household bills should be a priority over any debts you owe. Your major household bills should be a priority and paid first. This action is my suggested Hierarchy. Your priorities may be a little different, but should be like the following:

- Mortgage/Rent

- Gas, Electric & Water Utilities

- Telephone/Mobile Phones
- Internet/Cable
- Life Insurance
- Car Payments
- Auto Payments
- Credit Cards

As I mentioned on the previous page, technically tithing is no longer required, but you can still decide to tithe a certain amount of your income to God. What I want to reiterate is your giving or a request made by your church leaders should not put you in a position where you cannot handle your household expenses. God wants us to use wisdom and rightly divide the word of truth. Remember that God says those who love me keep my commandments. We are to care for God's local church buildings and the body of Christ in need. We do this by giving our income first fruits, tithes/offerings, and donations to our local church and other ministries or charities that God puts on your heart to give to. If we do this, God promises to open the windows of heaven and pour out a blessing, but there shall not be enough room to receive it. I am a witness!

Notes: Jot down words, sentences, or phrases that The Lord impresses upon your heart.

Commandment 2
Open an Emergency Fund & Savings Account

"Others said, "We have mortgaged our fields, vineyards, and homes to get food during the famine." ~Nehemiah 5:3

Emergency Fund

An emergency spending fund, often called an "emergency fund" or "rainy day fund," is a dedicated savings account or pool of money for unexpected and urgent financial needs or emergencies. The primary purpose of this fund is to provide a financial safety net, helping individuals or households cover unforeseen expenses without resorting to high-interest loans, using credit cards, or depleting other savings or investments.

Key characteristics of an emergency spending fund include:

- **Liquidity**: The funds in an emergency spending fund should be easily accessible and liquid, meaning they can be quickly converted to cash when needed. Familiar places to hold an emergency fund include savings accounts, money market accounts, or certificates of deposit (CDs) with short maturity periods.

- **Dedicated Purpose**: An emergency fund is specifically earmarked for unexpected expenses, such as medical bills, car repairs, home repairs, job loss, or other financial crises. It is not intended for regular or planned expenses like monthly bills or vacations.

- **Size**: The size of an emergency fund varies from person to person but typically ranges from three to six months worth of essential living expenses. Some financial experts recommend even more significant funds, depending on individual circumstances.

- **Security**: An emergency fund should be kept separate from everyday spending accounts and investments to maintain its intended purpose. This separation helps ensure that the fund remains available when needed most.

- **Regular Contributions**: Building and maintaining an emergency fund often involves making regular contributions from your income or windfall gains. Automated transfers or deposits can help individuals consistently grow their emergency fund.

- **No Risky Investments**: Emergency funds should not be invested in high-risk assets or subject to market volatility. The goal is to preserve the principal amount and have it readily available when emergencies arise.

An adequately funded emergency spending fund can provide peace of mind and financial stability during unexpected challenges. The fund allows individuals and families to weather economic storms without compromising long-term financial goals or accumulating high-interest debt.

The Bible says in Nehemiah 5:3 that God's People had to mortgage (take out a loan against) their fields, vineyards, and homes to get food during the famine. As people of God, we must be wise and plan for unexpected emergencies. Remember the COVID-19 pandemic? How many people were prepared for a catastrophe such as that? Although the pandemic went beyond one year, those who prepared by having an emergency fund were better able to manage the economic uncertainties that took place during that time, such as the loss of jobs, hospital and medical bills, and buying masks and other protective items. It is highly recommended that an emergency fund be established. Remember, an emergency fund is money saved in case of an emergency. It allows you to have access to funds to pay for unexpected emergencies such as an auto repair, medical bill, a fire, or job loss.

With how much should I begin saving?

Some experts suggest starting with saving at least 3-6 months of household expenses, but I suggest starting with any amount that you have. I do not care if you start save $5.00 each month. The goal is to get started saving right away. Everyone's amount will be different, but I would suggest having at least $500.00 - $1000.00 dollars in today's economy. Most singular occurrences of unexpected emergencies are rarely beyond that scale. You can start today. I encourage you to!

Earlier in this chapter, I laid out the term called Regular Contributions. One way to be consistent with building your emergency fund is to make contributions to the fund regularly. In today's online banking world, you can easily set up automatic deposits from a paycheck or monthly income into your checking account to move to your savings account. Many people like this "out of sight, out of mind" option because the money is usually deducted and transferred before you see it or begin paying other household bills from your checking account.

An adequately funded emergency fund can provide peace of mind and financial stability during unexpected challenges. The fund allows individuals and families to weather economic storms without compromising long-term financial goals or accumulating high-interest debt from credit cards, personal loans, or payday loans.

Regular Savings Accounts

Saving is for financial goals such a house, car, vacation, large appliances (refrigerator or washer & dryer), furniture, engagement rings and jewelry, computers and electronics, or tuition. Every savings account should have a label. This means that you must know what you are saving for or the savings account will be meaningless and vulnerable to premature withdrawals. For instance, set a financial goal to purchase a home computer for you and your family. And let's assume the computer will cost $800.00. Labeling and knowing what you are saving for will probably make you less likely to dip into the savings account and spend before you have reached the amount needed to meet your personal savings goal.

S.M.A.R.T. A smart goal is one that is specific, measurable, achievable, realistic, and time bound.

S - Well defined, clear, and unambiguous

M - With specific criteria that measure your progress toward the accomplishing of goal

A - Attainable and possible to achieve

R - Within reach, realistic, and relevant to your life purpose

T - With a clearly defined timeline, including a starting date and a target completion date. The purpose is to create urgency.

In the example above, the SMART goal will look like the following:

Specific: Save money to purchase a $800 HP 17, 17.3" Laptop on Amazon.com

Measurable: Save $100 each month for 6 months starting in January 2026

Attainable: Our family brings in enough monthly household income to buy a computer

Reasonable: Computer is to be used by our family for school and work

Time Bound: Purchase computer on June 30TH 2026

Are you paying yourself first?

Isn't it interesting that the average person works all their lives and never takes the time to consider paying themselves? Most parents are concerned about caring for their children and the bills, but we forget to pay ourselves first (after we give our first fruits to God).

There will always be bills to pay that will absorb our income and this is why we cannot wait for a "perfect" moment to save. Most savers have self-discipline, which is a fruit of

the Spirit and paying yourself first is a form of self-care. Saving takes away the worry and stress of "not having enough." The Bible says that the ants were wise and it behooves us to take a lesson from them. The ants work hard all summer storing food so they have plenty of provisions in the winter.

Saving and having reserves of money allows us to achieve and fund the vision that God gives to us for our lives and the lives of other believers. We are to finance the kingdom of God and be an example to the world because our God owns everything. The Bible says that the wealth of sinners is laid up for the righteous. When we obey the Biblical commandments about money, God will keep His promises to us. We will be the head and not the tail, we will be above and not beneath, we will be the lender, not the borrower. God will make grace abound and as we give unsparingly, God will bless us unsparingly. When we take care of the poor, the widowed, the orphaned, the elderly and those in need, God will take care of us!

Notes: Jot down words, sentences, or phrases that The Lord impresses upon your heart.

Commandment 3
Generate More Cash Flow

"But don't begin until you count the cost. For who would begin construction of a building without first calculating the cost to see if there is enough money to finish it?"
~Luke 14:28

Do you have cash flow? Cash flow is a term used in business. It is the movement of cash in and out of the business. It is a measure of a company's financial health. We can apply this same concept to our household income management (discussed in Chapter 1). Of course, the concept is simple; when a person always has cash, this implies that that person is doing well economically. Always having access to cash or assets is important. When you have positive cash flow, you are making enough money to cover your monthly household bills, possessing a funded emergency fund, and investing in mutual funds, stocks & bonds, digital coins, and rental properties. You can deposit money into your bank account and withdraw it without worrying that you will overdraft it.

When you have negative cash flow, you're not making enough money to cover your household expenses or other debt. Overdraft fees on your checking and savings accounts, late fees, over-the-limit fees on your credit card accounts, and late payments or partially paid bills are signs of Negative cash flow.

In my experience, most people pay all of their bills at a certain point in the month (usually the beginning when rent or mortgage is due) and have little to no money or cash flow until the next payday. I have also discovered that some people use a whole paycheck to pay their bills and another paycheck for personal shopping and spending. These practices strip a person of enjoying a financially free lifestyle. Positive cash flow is having cash no matter the day or month!

One solution to having cash flow always is to spread out your bills and expenses over the course of a month by matching the time when you receive your wages (income). For example, you can purchase a calendar to record your bills' due dates. Try to spread your bills throughout the month to ensure you have sufficient income to cover those bills each pay period.

For instance, assume you have a Mortgage note ($1800) due on the 1st day of the month, car payment ($350), auto insurance ($150), electric bill ($200), water bill ($100), and one credit card bill ($50) due on the 1st day of the month. These bills total $2650. If you receive a bi-weekly paycheck on the 1st for $2500, you are in the negative by $150 and have no cash flow until your next pay period. However, if you call your creditors to move your car payment ($350), auto insurance ($150), electric bill ($200), water bill ($100), and one credit card bill ($50) to the 15th day of month (bills totaling $850) you will have more "breathing room" because each pay period will leave you with discretionary income. You can then use the discretionary income as you wish, for example, use for a savings goal, to invest, to donate or to help others.

Most companies will accommodate you if you explain to them that you receive your income bi-weekly and need to change your due date. Note that most insurance companies bill you depending on when you purchase or renew a policy, so if at all possible, try to secure a policy or enter a contract on or around a date that works for you. This information is just one solution to having cash flow.

Another obvious solution is to live below your means. Let me personally use my household for an example; Currently one of our accounts has over $40,000.00 in it. I drive a used '04 BMW X3, and my husband drives a used '99 BMW 328i and an '08 Chevy Express Van-

both are in good condition. All our vehicles are paid for, so there are no car payments. Now of course we can afford to purchase a new vehicle if we choose to, but we like cash flow and would rather wait until we have enough money to either pay cash for our next upgraded vehicle or we will wait until we have the means to finance the car payments in a year or less.

Living below our means has kept us comfortable and stress free. You need to understand that although you can afford a purchase, does not mean that you should make that purchase. Why would my husband and I want to enter into a vehicle contract for six years and struggle to maintain those payments plus have to obtain a full coverage auto insurance policy on a financed vehicle? That is called bondage. The Israelites tried to escape that very issue. Serving a master (Pharoah) that treated them and their people harshly. **The Bible says, "But don't begin until you count the cost. For who would begin construction of a building without first calculating the cost to see if there is enough money to finish it?"** Some people want to appear as though they are doing well financially but in reality, they are slaves to their lenders. Going into deep debt, not living within or below your means, and overextending oneself financially can be extremely stressful and burdensome and can also lead to severe consequences such as judgments, liens, foreclosures and even filing for bankruptcy.

My husband jokes that some men look good driving in their new ride, but the payments, insurance, and maintenance are so expensive that the men cannot afford to take a lady out on a date-no cashflow. It appears they did not count the cost, LOL!

On another note, as a Christian woman of God (this applies to men too), God commands us to manage our finances wisely. According to Proverbs 31:16, a woman inspects and buys a field; with her earnings, plus she plants a vineyard. So apparently, this virtuous wife possessed cash flow to be able to purchase a garden. Further in the text, Proverbs 31:20 says she extends a helping hand to the poor and opens her arms to the needy.

How do you manage the finances that God has given you to care for your household and others who need a helping hand? We ought to consider our personal financial decisions and count the cost to ensure we are being good stewards of what God has given us, whether small or great.

Notes: Jot down words, sentences, or phrases that The Lord impresses upon your heart.

Commandment 4
Pull and Review Your Credit Report

"A church leader is a manager of God's household, so he must live a blameless life. He must not be arrogant or quick-tempered; he must not be a heavy drinker, violent, or dishonest with money."
~Titus 1:7

Let's begin this chapter by discussing what a credit report is. A credit report is a document that lists your financial behaviors from credit reporting agencies (Equifax, Experian & Trans Union) and keeps track of your financial history. A credit report displays how you borrow and repay your creditors (the people extending your credit). A credit report has four main sections:

- **Personal Information:** Personal information includes your name, address, and place of employment. This information is used to verify and identify you.

- **Account History:** Account history includes all your credit accounts and reports how you have paid these accounts or the contrary, how you have not paid. The accounts that you have paid are your positive

42

accounts and are considered paid satisfactorily. The accounts that you have paid unsatisfactorily are negative accounts. After a period of time (between 30-90 days), if these negative accounts continue to go unpaid, they are sent to collections and show in your report file as a debt collection account.

- **Public Records:** Public records display bankruptcies, judgments, tax liens, state and country court records, and child support. Bankruptcy represents financial failure and hardship. A judgment is a court order to pay a certain amount of money to a creditor who has filed a lawsuit against you. A tax lien is a lien imposed by law where a tax collector has the right to recover non-payment of taxes. They can file a claim against your personal property or assets to ensure the taxes are paid. Sometimes, the court orders that the money or taxes owed be seized (taken) from wages (paycheck) and paid through the employer. This action is known as garnishment. In fact, the law requires credit reporting agencies to include information about overdue child support in your credit report.

- **Credit Inquiries:** A credit inquiry lists all parties who accessed your credit report within the past two years. Some creditors access your credit report to see if you qualify or remain qualified for their programs or financial product offerings, such as credit cards.

You should review your credit report at least once a year. You can go to www.annualcreditreport.com to pull a free copy of your credit report from all three agencies once per year. **In Titus 1:7 The scripture teaches that a church leader (i.e., Deacon, Elder, Assistant Pastor, or Trustee) must live a blameless life since he or she has been tasked with managing God's household (the local church and ministries within that church).** A blameless life does not mean perfection, but a blameless life is of good character. The number one way a person's character was determined in biblical times, and now in the 21st century, is how a person keeps their word and pays their creditors back as agreed. For this reason, it is said that your credit report is your character on paper.

Luke 16:11 teaches, "And if you are untrustworthy with worldly wealth, who will trust you with the true riches of heaven?" That is a powerful verse! God is telling us that if we cannot manage our own money, how can we in good conscious manage the things of God? Yet, many church leaders in leadership positions have poor credit. Could it be a reason churches aren't growing financially & spiritually? Leaders should be held to a higher standard. God is saying, if we can't be trusted to manage $500, for example, how can we be trusted to manage $5000, or a 5 million dollar church budget?"

I have heard quite a few Christians pray to God for money, but we first must learn how to manage what is currently under our stewardship. If you have a bad credit report (late payments, going over your credit limit, stopped making your payments and accumulated huge debts) pray to God to help you find someone legitimate who can either help you repair and restore your credit report or save your money to hire a bankruptcy attorney. A bankruptcy has a stigma attached to it but a bankruptcy can give you a fresh start so you can get from under debt that is unmanageable. You have to start somewhere, and nothing will happen unless you take that first step to heal your finances.

Notes: Jot down words, sentences, or phrases that The Lord impresses upon your heart.

Commandment 5
Increase Your Credit Score

"Then God said, "I am El-Shaddai - 'God Almighty.' Be fruitful and multiply. You will become a great nation, even many nations. Kings will be among your descendants!"
~Genesis 35:11

Your credit score is based on a numerical calculation and examination of your personal credit history. This number reports your creditworthiness. Your credit score is primarily based on credit reporting information from the three main credit bureau agencies that we discussed in Chapter 4. Credit scoring is used prior to granting credit.

Creditors (the bank or institution supplying the credit or loan to you) review your credit report and look at your credit score to determine your risk level. The higher your credit score, the lower the risk you are. Contrarily, the lower your credit score, the higher your risk. With a high-risk level, banks are less likely to take a chance and extend credit or loans to you. Banks or institutions try to avoid a loss in revenue due to unpaid debts, and this is why they use your credit score to evaluate your potential risk level.

Lenders use credit scores to decide who qualifies

for a loan, at what interest rate, and at what credit limits. The higher your credit score, the better the interest rate you are offered when repaying loans or credit cards. Credit scoring is not limited to banks. Other organizations, such as mobile phone companies, insurance companies, employers, landlords, and government departments, use your credit score to determine your risk or character. For example, an employer like a bank will check your credit report before hiring you. The bank wants to see how well you repay your creditors because you would represent their financial institution. Remember, lenders such as banks provide loans (credit) to people with good credit scores. So naturally, a bank wants people with good credit scores to work for them. It would be contradictory for a bank to hire someone with inferior credit.

Your FICO Score:

Fair Isaac Corporation, also known as FICO, is the world's most widely used credit scoring system manager. FICO guidelines state that the following percentages make up a credit score:

- **Payment History:** This is about 35% of your score. Did you know that simply making your credit account payments on time makes up the highest percentage of your score?

- **Amounts Owed:** This is about 30% of your score. The FICO score is based on the amounts you owe on your credit accounts, the number of accounts you have (such as credit cards), and how much of your available credit you are using. The more you owe on your credit accounts, the lower your score will be.

- **Length of Credit History:** This is about 15% of score. Having credit accounts for a lengthy period of time (for example, 5, 10, 15 or 20 years) will increase your score. Although, you can obtain a high credit score with a short credit history if the rest of your credit report shows favorable credit management.

- **New Credit:** This is about 10% of your score. Applying for new credit or opening new credit accounts can decrease your credit score initially, especially if you apply for several different credit accounts. However, FICO distinguishes between a single loan and a search for many new credit lines. FICO does this in part by the length of time over which the inquiries occur. So, if you need a loan and are shopping to find the best rate, do it within a certain amount of time such as 30 days. This will avoid lowering your credit score.

- **Types of Credit Used:** This is about 10% of your score. Other minor factors can slightly increase your credit score such as having a balanced mix of credit accounts. A variation of credit cards, installment loans such as a mortgage and auto loan, and perspn loans can add to your score.

If you implement these practices, you will increase your credit score. If you have a low credit score, just remember that time and consistency will fix it.

NOTE: There is no quick fix to repairing and restoring credit. Obtaining a secured credit card is not the credit cure for all. A secured credit card will not always help or increase your score if you have a subpar credit history! If someone tells you different I would be cautious of that company or credit repair specialist. There exist some predatory credit repair programs that are highly priced and guarantee quick results but many times, they use unethical tactics that could get you into deeper financial (sometimes criminal) trouble.

Hey beloved, don't be discouraged by your negative accounts. Older negative accounts have less bearing on your credit score. What matters is what you do today! Did you know that creditors are more concerned with how you've been managing your credit over the last 12-24 months? This is true, so do better today...

If you have no credit, one of the quickest ways to obtain one is to apply for a department store credit card. If they will not give you credit, you can always obtain an unsecured credit card. An unsecured credit card is offered by a bank or creditor when you use your own cash deposit to initially fund (or secure) the credit card. Most secured credit cards will allow you to open an account for as low as $200. With timely payments, you can rebuild your credit.

In some situations, obtaining a secured credit card can help people re- establish their credit. **God commands us "to be fruitful and multiply,"** whether it is bearing godly children or using a talent or skill God has given you to make money. In Proverbs 31, the godly wife buys a garden to plant seeds that will grow fruits and vegetables so she can, in turn, feed her husband, family, and others in need. In today's global economy we need cash and credit to live and function. I like to say that cash is king and credit is queen. An excellent credit score can get you access to funds even when you do not have cash.

Ensure you try your best to maintain and increase your credit score using the prementioned methods. I will go further and suggest you do not co-sign for someone who cannot obtain their own credit accounts. Co-signing can leave you responsible for a debt if that person fails to make the payments on time regardless of if they agreed to pay. If no payment is made, it will leave a negative mark on your credit report and lower your credit score or worse! So, keep and protect a good score. God says, if you do this, "You will become a great nation (people/family). Kings & Queens will be among your descendants!"

Credit Score Scale

800-934 score	Excellent credit
720-799 score	Great credit
680-719 score	Good credit
620-679 score	Okay credit
580-619 score	Bad credit

Notes: Jot down words, sentences, or phrases that The Lord impresses upon your heart.

Commandment 6
Enroll in a Retirement Plan

"Take a lesson from the ants, you lazybones. Learn from their ways and become wise! Though they have no prince or governor or ruler to make them work, they labor hard all summer, gathering food for the winter."
~Proverb 6:6-8

A retirement plan account is a specialized financial account designed to help individuals save and invest for their retirement. These accounts offer tax advantages and are intended to provide income during retirement when individuals are no longer actively earning a regular paycheck. Employers, financial institutions (including banks), or government programs can offer retirement plan accounts, and they come in various forms to suit diverse needs and circumstances. The following pages will discuss these accounts.

TYPES OF RETIREMENT ACCOUNTS

- **IRA (Individual Retirement Account)**: IRAs are personal retirement accounts that individuals can set up independently. There are two primary types of IRAs: Traditional IRAs and Roth IRAs. The main difference between Roth and Traditional IRA plans is when taxes are applied.

In a traditional IRA, contributions are made pre-tax (this helps reduce your tax liability at the end of the year when filing your tax return). As long as you do not make any withdrawals from the traditional account, no taxes are owed. Taxes become due when you make a withdrawal or receive a distribution from your traditional account. The amount of tax due depends on your age, but again, with a Traditional IRA, you don't pay now, but you will pay later. Whereas in a Roth IRA, contributions are taxed up front (but the withdrawals are tax-free). More people are considering Roth IRA accounts as an alternative to traditional plans. IRA is the general name for types of accounts that are used for retirement whether sponsored by your employer or you open an account individually.

- **401(k) Plan**: A 401(k) plan is a specific type of IRA account. These are employer-sponsored retirement plans offered to employees, typically in the private sector. Employees contribute a portion of their

  salary to the plan, and employers may match a portion of those contributions. 401(k) plans offer tax benefits, and contributions are invested in a variety of investment options chosen by the employee.

- **SEP-IRA (Simplified Employee Pension Individual Retirement Account)**: These are retirement accounts for self-employed individuals and small business owners. Employers contribute to these IRAs on behalf of eligible employees including themselves.

- **SIMPLE IRA (Savings Incentive Match Plan for Employees)**: These are retirement plans for small businesses, designed to be easy to administer. Both employers and employees make contributions to these IRAs.

- **Pension Plans**: Some employers offer traditional pension plans, also known as defined benefit plans. These plans promise a specific retirement benefit based on salary and years of service. Employers are responsible for funding and managing these plans.

- **Government-Sponsored Plans:** Government entities offer retirement plans, such as the Federal Thrift Savings Plan (TSP) for federal employees or state- specific pension plans for government workers.

Having a retirement plan account is significant for several reasons:

- **Financial Security in Retirement**: Retirement accounts allow individuals to accumulate savings over time, providing a source of income when they stop working and during their retirement years.

- **Tax Benefits**: As previously stated, many retirement accounts offer tax advantages, such as tax-deferred growth or tax-free withdrawals, which can help individuals maximize their savings.

- **Employer Contributions**: Employer-sponsored plans, like 401(k)s, often include employer matches, which can significantly boost retirement savings.

- **Long-Term Financial Goals**: Retirement accounts encourage long-term financial planning, helping individuals build a nest egg to support themselves in retirement and leave an inheritance for their heirs.

- **Financial Independence**: A retirement plan can reduce reliance on government social programs or benefits, providing a sense of financial independence.

Choosing a retirement plan that aligns with your financial goals, risk tolerance, and individual circumstances is essential. Regular contributions and prudent investment decisions can help ensure a more comfortable and financially secure retirement.

The earlier you begin planning and saving for

retirement, the more financial resources you'll have available when you retire. This long-term approach offers several benefits:

- **Compound Growth**: By starting early, your investments have more time to grow through the power of compounding, where your earnings generate additional earnings over time.

- **Lower Risk**: With a longer investment horizon, you can afford to take on more risk in your investment portfolio, potentially leading to higher returns.

- **Stress-Free Retirement**: Accumulating wealth over time eases financial stress in retirement, allowing you to maintain your desired lifestyle and cover essential expenses.

- **Flexibility**: Early savers have more flexibility in choosing retirement dates and can enjoy more options for how they spend their retirement years.

- **Legacy Planning**: Saving long-term enables you to leave a legacy for loved ones or support charitable causes.

The Bible says that it behooves us to take notes and observe how the ants ensure they have a safeguarded winter by harvesting in the summer. We can apply this same concept now by making wise decisions and investing today, resulting in a more secure future for not only us, but for future generations.

Do not allow the lower power (Satan) to make you feel guilty, anxious, or ashamed about past financial decisions where we either started late or have not started at all. Beloved, do not forget that you have today and it is never too early or late to start planning and saving for retirement. Even small contributions over time can significantly impact your financial security during your retirement years.

Notes: Jot down words, sentences, or phrases that The Lord impresses upon your heart.

Commandment 7

Homeownership (Buy a Home)

"A house is built by wisdom and becomes strong through good sense. Through knowledge its rooms are filled with all sorts of precious riches and valuables."
~Proverbs 24:3-4

Homeownership refers to the state of owning a residential property, typically a house or condominium, where an individual or family holds legal title to the property, providing them with the rights and responsibilities of maintaining and residing in the dwelling. Homeownership is the largest investment that most people will make during their lives.

Benefits of Home Ownership

Homeownership offers several advantages, including the potential for building equity and wealth over time, as property values often appreciate. It provides stability, allowing homeowners to establish roots in a community and enjoy a sense of ownership. Additionally, mortgage payments contribute to forced savings, while tax benefits may reduce home ownership costs.

Homeowners can also personalize their space; in the long term, their property can serve as a valuable asset for retirement or generational wealth transfer.

Categories for Home Ownership

Homes can be categorized in various ways based on their type, style, size, and function. All of these different types of homes have home ownership benefits. Here are some common types of dwellings:

- **Single-Family Home**: A single-family home is a stand-alone dwelling designed for one family, typically with its yard and walls not shared with neighboring homes.

- **Condominium (Condo)**: A condo is an individually owned unit within a multi-unit building or complex, with shared common areas and maintenance responsibilities.

- **Townhouse**: A multi-level, attached home that shares walls with neighboring units, typically arranged in rows.

- **Duplex**: A building with two separate living units, often side by side or one on top of the other. This is a great way to pay for your mortgage while renting the secondary unit. Most recommended if this is a livable and available option.

- **Mobile Home**: A mobile home is a prefabricated, transportable dwelling designed for mobile living, often in manufactured home parks.

- **Tiny House**: A tiny home is a compact and minimalistic home designed for simplified living, usually with a small footprint.

- **Cooperative (Co-op):** a cooperative is when residents own shares in a corporation that owns the building, and in return, they have the right to occupy a specific unit.

- **Bungalow**: A single-story is a small to medium-sized home with a characteristic low-pitched roof and front porch.

- **Mansion**: A mansion is a large and luxurious residence, often associated with wealth and prestige.

- **Ranch**: A ranch is a single-story home with a long, ground-level layout, typically with an open floor plan.

- **Cabin/Cottage**: A cabin/cottage is a small, rustic dwelling, often in rural or scenic areas, used for vacation or weekend getaways.

- **Villa**: A villa is a large, upscale home often associated with a Mediterranean or Spanish architectural style.

- **Colonial**: A colonial is a home inspired by the colonial architecture of early American settlers, typically featuring symmetry and rectangular shapes.

No matter your choice or style, buying a home allows you to build equity (the difference between the value of your home and the balance that is owed on your home mortgage). For example: You purchased a home in 2020 for $200,000 paid your mortgage for 7 years and the home is now worth $275,000. The equity in your home would be $75,000. You can pull out that equity by refinancing your loan. After refinancing, you can use that equity to pay off credit cards and other debt, do upgrades to the home (new HVAC system, modernize kitchen or bathroom, add new siding or invest in solar panels), invest in higher education or your child(s) 529 College Savings Plan, jumpstart your IRA account, invest in digital coin or stocks & bonds, invest in a rental property, or you can do a combination of things-there are endless opportunities. The goal is to use the cash in a way that will position you in the best financial situation possible.

Advantages of Renting Versus Buying

RENTER:

- Unpredictable increased rent payment or fees

- No or low maintenance (not responsible for mowing grass, snow removal, and others)

- No property taxes

- Flexibility and feasibility of relocation or change of address

- Access to amenities (fitness and weight room and laundry room

- Lower insurance costs (some cases rental insurance is optional although I do not suggest opting out)

HOMEOWNER:

- Unsurprising monthly payments and lower than renting in the long term

- Responsible for maintenance and upkeep of home (inside and outside) including water, sewer, and electric

- Real estate & property taxes

- Non-flexibility of moving or relocating (may take some time to sell a home)

- Responsible for large appliance purchase, HVAC and home warranties coverage

Notes: Jot down words, sentences, or phrases that The Lord impresses upon your heart.

Commandment 8
Create Wealth

"He did all this so you would never say to yourself, 'I have achieved this wealth with my own strength and energy.' Remember the LORD your God. He is the one who gives you power to be successful, in order to fulfill the covenant that He confirmed to your ancestors with an oath."
~Deuteronomy 8:17-18

Wealth creation refers to the process of accumulating financial assets and resources over time, typically to achieve long-term financial security, increase one's net worth, and improve one's overall economic well-being.

This process involves various strategies such as saving, investing, and making prudent financial decisions to generate income and build assets that grow in value. Wealth creation can result from income from work, investments, business ownership, and real estate appreciation. It often involves setting and working towards financial goals to create a more comfortable and prosperous future. Wealth creation is important for several reasons. Let us review them.

- **Financial Security**: Accumulating wealth provides a safety net, helping individuals and families weather unexpected financial challenges, such as medical emergencies or job loss.

- **Retirement Planning**: Building wealth is crucial for a secure retirement. It ensures that individuals can maintain their desired lifestyle and cover expenses when they stop working.

- **Achieving Goals**: Wealth creation allows people to achieve personal and financial goals, whether it's buying a home, funding education, starting a business, or traveling the world.

- **Generational Wealth**: It enables the transfer of assets and financial advantages to future generations, providing opportunities and security for one's heirs.

- **Reducing Financial Stress**: A strong financial position reduces stress and anxiety associated with money, leading to improved overall well-being.

- **Independence and Freedom**: Wealth grants individuals greater control over their lives and choices, offering the freedom to pursue passions, career changes, and philanthropic endeavors.

- **Investment in the Future**: Wealth creation often involves investments in the local economy and businesses, contributing to economic growth and job creation.

- **Philanthropy**: Accumulated wealth can be used to support charitable causes and make a positive impact on society.

Wealth creation empowers individuals to live life on their terms and leaves a lasting legacy. It's not just about accumulating money but also about achieving financial stability, fulfilling personal aspirations, making a positive impact on one's life BUT especially in the lives of others. Our money is not just to be used for our own gain and comfortable life, but to be able to provide for the needs of the impoverished children, women, widows, and neighbors.

Wealth creation goes further when we are speaking in terms of Kingdom Business. We have to be about our Father's business. As Jehovah Jireh (Provider) provides us with wealth, we are responsible for sharing and getting a portion of our wealth into the hands of the poor, needy, orphaned, and widowed. Our wealth can be used to bless individual lives, but it can also be used to promote a cause or social struggle. It can be used in support of a nationwide or worldwide biblical ministry which feeds communities of people not only physical bread, but more importantly; the bread of life-Jesus. God says, "And the Good News about the kingdom will be preached throughout the whole world, so that all nations (people) shall hear it; and then the end will come."

The Bible further states that money is a necessity. It is a means to an end. Meaning, money is used initially to motivate and provide but the end is all about everyone hearing the gospel of Christ so that they can chose (or not) to believe on Him, live a life dedicated to Him, and be witnesses to all so that the hope is that none would perish, but all have everlasting life. So, wealth creation, and being responsible over what finances God has entrusted us goes way deeper than simply taking care of our needs and wants.

We cannot take for granted that God gives us the ability to create wealth because creating wealth is tied to another promise of God. God is not a man that He would lie or the son of man (a human) that He would repent. These scriptures at the beginning of each chapter are part of God's holy purpose and plan. We have to obey these commandments, statutes, and principals the same way that we keep the commandment that says, "We shall not kill or bear false witness (tell lies) against our neighbors." We cannot be selective about the scriptures we choose to obey and not obey and that includes scriptures about money and our stewardship over it.

You know, I once heard it said that poor people work for their money while rich people have their money work for them. That being said, here are some common investments that can make your money grow over time:

- ***Stock** - Investing in stocks means buying shares in a company, representing ownership in that business. Each stock share has a specific price, like Coca-Cola, which may be priced at $35.00 per share. For instance, if you acquire two shares of Coca- Cola stock, your total investment amounts to $70.00 ($35.00 x 2 shares). When a company, such as Coca-Cola, performs well and generates more profits, its stock price typically rises. For example, if the Coca-Cola share price increases to $40.00 per share, your portfolio value becomes $80.00 ($40.00 x 2 shares). Resulting in a gross gain of $10. Stock invests in only one particular company and the risk or reward is in how well that company generates revenue. If you invest in only one stock (putting all of your eggs in one basket), you are susceptible to a greater loss or reward. Once you have a loss, there is no recovering your initial investment.

Stock is the riskiest type of investment depending on what you are investing in.

- ***Mutual Fund** - A mutual fund is an investment vehicle that pools money from multiple investors to hire a professional manager responsible for investing in a diversified portfolio of stocks, bonds, and various securities on behalf of the investors. Investing in a mutual fund is investing in more than one company and theoretically, the purpose is to reduce your overall risk when one company is not doing well. For instance, in the previous example Coca-Cola drops its per share value to $30 per share. Resulting in a $10 loss ($5 x 2 shares), but in this case, you own Coca-Cola and Apple stock and the Apple stock does very well, so in this case, you do not feel the loss because what Apple stock gained absorbed the value of what you loss (in a sense).

- ***Bonds** - A bond is a debt instrument, similar to an IOU, where you lend money to a government or corporation in exchange for a bond. Bonds promise to pay a specified interest rate over a designated period, offering a way to earn income while investing in entities like governments or corporations. Bond terms can range from 6 months to several years. It's a safer investment because you know exactly how much of a return you will receive at the end of the term. For example, a $500 U.S. Savings bond, earning 6% interest, held for 1 year, compounded monthly by a person in the 22% federal tax bracket would earn $23.75 per the Treasury Direct website as of August 2024. Please note that some bonds are guaranteed and some have a variable rate of interest that is tied to inflation.

- ***Certificate of Deposit (CD)** - A Certificate of Deposit is a financial product available through banks and credit unions. It resembles a savings account but involves lending your money to the institution for a predetermined period. In exchange, the bank usually provides a higher interest rate

  as compensation. (Similar to bonds but you are loaning your money to a bank).

- ***Cryptocurrencies** - Are digital currencies not backed by real assets or tangible securities. They are traded between consenting parties with no broker and tracked on digital ledgers. An example of a specific digital coin company is Bitcoin. There are other types of cryptocurrency companies to invest in. Investing in Crypto can have a downside because it can be very volatile and drop significantly, which puts an investor at a higher risk of losing their investment but on the contrary, digital currency can have higher and faster gains as well! Choose wisely.

*DISCLAIMER: Please note that all investments come with inherent risks and assessing your personal risk tolerance is prudent. Before making any investment decisions, seeking guidance from a qualified and licensed financial advisor is strongly advisable. This book does not endorse or promote any specific investments; instead, its purpose is solely to offer educational definitions and information.

Notes: Jot down words, sentences, or phrases that The Lord impresses upon your heart.

Commandment 9
Protect Your Family with Insurance

"A prudent person foresees danger and takes precautions. The simpleton goes blindly on and suffers the consequences."
~Proverbs 27:12

Insurance is a crucial safeguard for your assets, shielding you from various risks that life can bring. It protects against everyday mishaps like auto accidents, unexpected illnesses, and theft and extends coverage for rare and catastrophic events such as fires, floods, or even loss of life. Documenting your possessions with photos and retaining receipts can help substantiate expenses in the event of unexpected incidents, making the recovery process smoother.

Furthermore, insurance goes beyond asset protection; it offers invaluable benefits:

- **Financial Security**: Insurance provides a safety net, ensuring that you and your family can withstand the economic impact of unforeseen events, reducing the burden of unexpected expenses.

- **Peace of Mind**: Knowing you are covered in

times of crisis brings peace of mind, relieving stress and allowing you to focus on recovery.

- **Debt Settlement**: In the unfortunate event of your passing, insurance can settle debts, easing the financial burden on your loved ones and ensuring they are provided for.

Different Insurances

Different types of insurance are essential components of financial awareness, each serving unique purposes. They act as a safety net, mitigating financial risks and ensuring that individuals and families can maintain their financial well-being in the face of unexpected events. Additionally, insurance encourages responsible financial planning by promoting the prudent management of risks, ultimately contributing to long-term financial security.

- **Health Insurance:** Vital for covering medical expenses. It ensures access to quality healthcare without the fear of high bills.

- **Auto Insurance:** Mandatory in many places, it protects against vehicle-related accidents and liabilities, ensuring you're financially responsible on the road.

- **Homeowners/Renters Insurance:** Safeguards your home or belongings against theft, damage, or disasters, preserving your property and personal assets.

- **Life Insurance:** Offers financial protection to your family in the event of your demise, helping settle debts, cover funeral costs, and maintain their economic well-being.

- **Whole Life Insurance:** Whole life insurance is another type of life insurance that usually lasts your entire life. It also includes a cash value element that grows over time. Once you've earned enough cash value, you can use it to take out a loan, pay your premiums and more. As long as you pay your premiums and stay current you can access these benefits.

- **Universal Life Insurance** is a form of permanent life insurance that gives policyholders flexibility. These flexible terms include options on paying premiums (generally the premiums are less expensive than Whole Life but more expensive than Term), they include a cash savings component, and a death benefit. Universal life insurance allows you to borrow against policy or cash in your savings portion, which grows tax-deferred over your lifetime.

- **Indexed Universal Life Insurance** is a type of permanent coverage, which means it can last your entire life and build cash value. Unlike other types of universal life, an IUL policy places the cash value in sub-accounts that mirror the stock market indexes (Such as the Dow Jones, NASDAQ, or the S&P 500). As an alternative to indexed accounts (often a type of mutual fund), IUL policies also offer fixed account options that earn interest at a set rate. Unlike investing directly in an index fund, you won't lose money when the market has a downturn.

- **Disability Insurance:** Provides income replacement if you become disabled and cannot work, ensuring you can still meet your financial commitments.

- **Property Insurance (e.g., Fire, Flood):** Property insurance covers losses to your property due to natural disasters, mitigating the financial impact of unexpected events.

- **Liability Insurance:** Shields you from legal liabilities and potential lawsuits, safeguarding your assets and financial stability.

- **Business Insurance:** Business insurance is vital for entrepreneurs. This insurance protects business assets and income, ensuring continuity in the face of unexpected challenges.

On another note, may I ask, how many times have you heard about a family that didn't have insurance for a burial, cremation, or memorial service for their loved one? How many times have you or someone you know was part of an automobile accident but the driver was not covered or lapsed on their insurance premium, unable to repair or replace their vehicle, causing a transportation issue? How many times have you either lost, dropped, damaged, or had your cell phone stolen but no phone coverage and as a result, had to pay full price for a new one. The Bible says a prudent man or woman sees danger and takes precautions. Insurance is a type of preparation and precaution. We sometimes treat insurance as a luxury or non-necessity, and although insurance is often offered as an "add on' and non-mandatory, I would warn you against not having insurance. Any type of insurance is a wise decision that can prevent emotional and financial stress. Having insurance can help you to navigate the uncertainties of life and offer you peace of mind and security when unexpected emergencies, tragedies, or disasters occur. If you have ever been an iPhone owner with Apple phone insurance, and need a repair, I would call your attention to the different experiences and benefits that you will encounter if you do carry their phone coverage protections. For example, you get moved to the front of the line and do not have to wait for an appointment. The first time I experienced this, I felt and was treated like a VIP

(Very Important Person). Having insurance absolutely makes life easier and takes the frustration out of an already trying or difficult time. When I lost my dear mother, having insurance allowed me to focus on fulfilling my mother's last wishes. I will say this, "A small sacrifice reaps a large harvest." Be wise.

*DISCLAIMER: Before purchasing any insurance policy, seeking guidance from a qualified and licensed insurance agent or a licensed financial advisor is strongly advisable. This book does not endorse or promote any specific insurance product or policy; instead, its purpose is solely to offer educational definitions and information.

Notes: Jot down words, sentences, or phrases that The Lord impresses upon your heart.

Commandment 10
Prepare a Will and/or Trust

"Good people leave an inheritance to their grandchildren, but the sinner's wealth passes to the godly." ~Proverbs 13:22

Estate
Did you know that all of the property of a living or deceased person (such as homes, cars, rental properties, jewelry, intellectual property, social media accounts, art, stocks, bonds, digital currency, and other investments & assets) are part of what is called an Estate?

Estate Planning
Estate Planning is the process of planning how an individual's assets will be arranged, managed, preserved, transferred, distributed or disposed after death. Estate Planning is typically completed while a person is still living and the goal is to plan as early as possible especially while a person is coherent. It is best to plan as early as you acquire assets of value, or assets that meet the requirement in value based on the State laws that a person lives in. For example, in the state of Delaware, when a person dies, with assets over $30K, the heirs and/or beneficiaries must open what is called an Estate.

A Testate Estate vs Intestate Estate

A testate estate means that the decedent (deceased person) left a will, which outlines how his or her property will be distributed and to which parties it will be distributed. An intestate estate means that the decedent did not leave a will and the probate court will determine the distribution of his or her property to heirs according to a priority statute.

Testate

The advantages of dying with a Will or Estate Package (Testate) outweigh the disadvantages of dying without a Will. For one, when you die and leave a Will, you make your wishes and other details known so that your loved ones or the State (in some cases) won't be left to determine what you would have wanted to happen to your assets and other property. Another advantage is the family does not have to argue about who gets what. You can settle that in your Will and when your Will is legally prepared, it is final. Who can argue with a dead person? Another advantage of Estate Planning and dying in testate is that the family does not have to come up with money to bury or cremate you. Most people who draft a Will are responsible and have most likely purchased life insurance to cover death expenses.

Intestate

The disadvantage of dying intestate is obvious especially if you have accumulated any assets such as a home, a vehicle, cash, stock shares and other investments. One disadvantage is family conflicts. I am sure you know someone who has died intestate and the extremely intense and sometimes detrimental disagreements, debates, arguments and more! It is bad enough to battle with family members over property but imagine having to battle with the probate court. Probate means the official proving of a Will. Probate court is the government or power which has the authority to oversee the handling of Estates and ensure that a Will is properly administrated and executed. When a person dies intestate (no Will), and they have assets that have minimum value according to the laws of each state (check your local office of the Register of Wills for more information) the probate court decides how the person's property and estate will be divided and/or distributed. Usually, the probate court and Register of Wills has a hierarchy which they use as a guideline to disperse assets to heirs. For example, the Spouse of the deceased person is first in line, then the children if there is no spouse, or the spouse is deceased, then the grandchildren and etcetera.

Will

A Will and a Trust are both estate planning tools, but they serve different purposes and can work together to create a comprehensive estate plan. A Will is a legally binding document that outlines an individual's wishes regarding the distribution of their assets, property, and belongings after their passing. It is a critical component of financial awareness because as we discussed, it ensures that a person's financial affairs are managed according to their preferences, minimizing disputes among heirs and potential legal complications. A well-structured Will can help protect and efficiently transfer one's wealth, assets, and financial legacy, providing clarity and peace of mind to both the individual and their beneficiaries.

Trust

A Trust is a legal arrangement where one party (the trustor or grantor) transfers ownership of assets to another party (the trustee) to hold and manage for the benefit of specific individuals or entities (the beneficiaries). Trusts are essential in terms of financial awareness for several reasons. They offer a structured way to protect and manage assets, facilitate the efficient transfer of wealth, and minimize estate taxes.

Trusts can provide for beneficiaries' financial needs while allowing for specific conditions or instructions to be met. They also offer privacy and can expedite the distribution of assets, helping individuals maintain control over their financial legacy while ensuring their wishes are honored.

Revocable & Irrevocable Trust

A revocable trust allows you to retain control over your assets during your lifetime and make changes or revoke the trust if needed.

An irrevocable trust, once established, typically cannot be altered or revoked by the grantor, offering asset protection and potential estate tax advantages but requiring a relinquishment of control over the assets placed in the trust.

The Connection Between the Will & the Trust

The connection between them often involves the use of a "Pour-Over Will." This type of Will is used to ensure that any assets not already placed in the Trust during your lifetime are transferred into the Trust upon your death. In essence, the Pour-Over Will acts as a safety net to catch any assets that may have been inadvertently left out of the Trust.

Benefits of Burying the Will in the Trust

- **Privacy**: When assets are placed in a trust, the details of those assets and their distribution typically remain private. In contrast, a will becomes part of the public record during probate, allowing anyone to access information about your estate.

- **Efficient Asset Transfer**: Assets held within a trust can bypass the probate process, which can be time-consuming and costly. This action means that beneficiaries can typically access their inheritances more quickly.

- **Avoiding Probate Costs**: Probate proceedings often involve legal fees and court costs, which can erode the value of your estate. Placing assets in a trust can help avoid or minimize these expenses.

- **Control and Flexibility**: Trusts allow for more control over the distribution of assets, including specifying conditions or timelines for distributions to beneficiaries. This control can be valuable for individuals with complex family situations or specific wishes.

- **Minimizing Estate Taxes**: Certain types of trusts, such as irrevocable trusts, can help minimize estate taxes, benefiting you and your heirs.

- **Continuity of Management**: In the event of your incapacity, a well- structured trust can ensure the seamless management and distribution of your assets, avoiding the need for court- appointed conservators or guardians.

- **Protection of Minor Beneficiaries**: Trusts can provide for the financial needs of minor beneficiaries while designating a trustee to manage and distribute assets on their behalf until they reach a specified age or meet certain conditions.

- **Legacy Planning**: Trusts can be instrumental in crafting a lasting legacy, whether by supporting charitable causes or providing for future generations, allowing your influence and financial support to extend beyond your lifetime.

In summary, while a Will and a Trust serve distinct roles in estate planning, they can complement each other to create a comprehensive strategy. Burying the Will in the Trust, along with properly funding and managing the Trust during your lifetime, offers benefits such as privacy, efficient asset transfer, cost savings, and greater control over the distribution of assets, contributing to a well- rounded estate plan. Incorporating a Trust into your estate planning strategy adds an extra layer of security and organization to your financial affairs, ensuring that your wishes are carried out efficiently and according to your specific intentions.

Talk to your local Register of Wills to get more information on this topic.

Notes: Jot down words, sentences, or phrases that The Lord impresses upon your heart.

Additional Financial Terms

- **Spending Habits:** This refers to the patterns and behaviors people exhibit when using their income. It can describe whether someone spends money frugally, extravagantly, wisely, or impulsively.

- **Spending Plan or Budget:** Creating a spending plan or budget involves allocating your income to different categories of expenses, savings, and investments. It helps individuals manage their finances effectively.

- **Spending Power:** This term reflects how much purchasing capability your income provides. Higher income generally means greater spending power, allowing for more significant purchases and financial choices.

- **Spending Rate:** The spending rate indicates the portion of your income you use or consume regularly. The spending rate can be measured on a daily, weekly, monthly, or yearly basis.

- **Spending Priorities:** Your income can be allocated based on your priorities, with some people emphasizing spending on necessities like housing and food. In contrast, others prioritize discretionary expenditures in hobbies or travel.

- **Spending Capacity:** This refers to your ability to spend or make purchases without exceeding your income or budget constraints. It's essential for maintaining financial stability.

- **Overspending:** This term describes spending more money than your income allows, leading to potential financial difficulties and debt.

- **Spending Review:** Periodically reviewing your spending helps you assess whether you are staying within your budget and identify areas where adjustments may be needed.

- **Spending Limits:** Setting limits on how much you can spend in specific categories or during certain periods helps you control your expenses and avoid financial strain.

- **Spending Patterns: Examining your** past spending behavior can reveal trends and tendencies that impact your financial health.

- **Spending Decision:** Any choice you make

regarding how to use your income, whether for necessities, savings, investments, or discretionary purchases, can be considered a spending decision.

- **Spending Responsibly:** This concept emphasizes using your income in a manner that aligns with your financial goals, avoids unnecessary debt, and supports long-term economic well-being.

- **Employment**: Wages, salaries, and bonuses earned through work or work- related activities.

- **Investments**: Returns on investments such as stock dividends, interest from savings accounts or bonds, and capital gains from selling assets.

- **Business Activities**: Profit generated from running a business or self- employment, which includes revenue minus expenses.

- **Rental Income**: Payments from renting out real estate properties or assets to others.

- **Retirement Benefits**: Income received during retirement, including pensions, Social Security, or distributions from retirement accounts like 401(k)s or IRAs.

- **Government Assistance**: Payments from

government programs like unemployment, welfare, or disability benefits.

- **Royalties and Licensing**: Earnings from licensing intellectual property, such as copyrights, patents, or trademarks.

- **Alimony and Child Support**: Money received as part of legal agreements for spousal or child support.

- **Financial Awareness:** A spending plan provides a clear and detailed overview of the family's income and expenses. It helps members understand where their money is coming from and where it's going, promoting financial awareness.

- **Expense Control**: By tracking expenses, a spending plan allows families to identify areas where they may be overspending or where costs can be reduced. It helps in controlling unnecessary or impulsive spending.

- **Savings Goals**: A spending plan helps families allocate funds toward specific savings goals, such as emergencies, education, retirement, or a vacation. It ensures that money is set aside regularly to achieve these objectives.

- **Debt Management**: Families with debts, such as credit card debt, loans, or mortgages, can use a spending plan to create a strategy for paying off these obligations efficiently. It prevents the accumulation of additional debt.

- **Income Management**: It ensures that the family's income is effectively managed, covering essential expenses while allowing for discretionary spending and savings. Income management helps prevent financial stress and unexpected shortfalls.

- **Financial Stability**: A well-structured spending plan promotes financial stability by ensuring the family's expenses do not exceed their income. It prevents living paycheck to paycheck and helps build a financial cushion.

- **Emergency Preparedness:** Having a spending plan in place ensures that funds are available to handle unexpected expenses or emergencies, reducing the need to rely on high-interest loans or credit cards.

- **Long-Term Financial Goals**: Families can use a spending plan to work toward long-term financial goals, such as buying a home, funding a child's education, or retiring comfortably. It provides a roadmap for achieving these aspirations.

- **Communication**: Creating a spending plan encourages open communication within the family regarding financial goals, priorities, and decisions. It promotes unity

  in financial matters and reduces conflicts.

- **Financial Accountability**: A spending plan holds family members accountable for their financial responsibilities. Each member can have a role in managing the budget and ensuring financial goals are met.

- **Future Planning**: Families can use a spending plan to project future financial scenarios, such as how changes in income or expenses may impact their financial situation over time. These actions help in long-term planning.

- **Peace of Mind**: Having a spending plan provides peace of mind. It reduces financial stress, helps families feel more in control of their finances, and provides a sense of security.

- **Dedicated Purpose**: An emergency fund is specifically earmarked for unexpected expenses, such as medical bills, car repairs, home repairs, job loss, or other financial crises. It is not intended for regular or planned expenses like monthly bills or vacations.

- **Size**: The size of an emergency fund varies from person to person but typically ranges from three to six months' worth of essential living expenses. Some financial experts recommend even more significant funds, depending on individual circumstances.

- **Security**: An emergency fund should be kept separate from everyday spending accounts and investments to maintain its intended purpose. This separation helps ensure that the fund remains available when needed most.

- **Regular Contributions**: Building and maintaining an emergency fund often involves making regular contributions from your income or windfall gains. Automated transfers or deposits can help

  individuals consistently grow their emergency fund.

- **No Risky Investments**: Emergency funds should not be invested in high-risk assets or subject to market volatility. The goal is to preserve the principal amount and have it readily available when emergencies arise.

RESOURCES

For a **free copy of your credit report** from all three credit agencies once per year visit **www.annualcreditreport.com**

For **Fair Isaac Corporation** (developed the FICO score and used for the credit score in most mortgage applications) visit **www.myfico.com**

For **Fair Credit Reporting Act**: A law that regulates and protects the rights, fairness, accuracy, and privacy of the consumer's personal information contained in the files of the credit reporting agencies visit **www.ftc.gov**

Money tools for kids: **www.kids.gov**

To find a secured or unsecured credit card with rate comparisons visit **www.bankrate.com**

Credit Agencies:
- www.equifax.com
- www.experian.com
- www.transunion.com

FURTHER RECOMMENDED READING & WEBSITE BROWSING

Lynette Khalfani-Cox – Your First Million
The Money Coach's Guide to Your First Million unfolds Lynnette's unique, seven step plan with strategies to help you manage money, pay off debt, build a great credit rating, and work towards growing and preserving wealth.

Robert Kiyosaki – Rich Dad Poor Dad
In the book Robert discusses his two fathers: his biological father, the poor dad and the other was the father of his childhood best friend, Mike the rich dad. Both fathers taught the author how to achieve success but with very disparate approaches. It became evident to the author which father's approach made more financial sense. Throughout the book, the author compares both fathers, their principles, ideas, financial practices, and degree of dynamism.

Suze Orman – Financial Guidebook
In this book, Suze Orman investigates the dysfunctional relationship women have with money.

Dave Ramsey – Financial Peace
In this book, Ramsey gives financial advice based on his personal experience instead of what he learned in a classroom.

The Budgetnista, Personal Financial Educator & Get Good With Money by Tiffany Aliche (2022)
Website: TheBudgetnista.com

Economic Empowerment, Finance and Investment by Dr. Boyce Watkins, Social Influencer
Website: BoyceWatkins.com

What to Do with Your Money When Crisis Hits: A Survival Guide by Michelle Singletary, Columnist, (2024)
Website: MichelleSingletary.com

Dave Ramsey, Christian Financial Advisor
Website: DaveRamseySolutions.com

Rich Dad, Poor Dad by Robert Kiyosaki (2023) Website: RichDad.com

Rianka R. Dorsainvil & Lazetta Rainey Braxton, CEO's of Financial Planning & Wealth Management
Website: 2050WealthPartners.com

MJ's Favorite Money Quotes

"We can tell our values by looking at our checkbook stubs."
~ Gloria Steinem

"A bank is a place that will lend you money if you can prove that you do not need it."
~ Bob Hope

"The art of living easily as to money is to pitch your scale of living one degree below your means."
~ Sir Henry Taylor

"It's not more money we need, we need better money management."
~ Marcella Joanne "MJ" Haskins

"Money is kind of a base subject. like water, food, air and housing, it affects everything yet for some reason the world of academics thinks it's a subject below their social standing." **&**

"We go to school to learn to work hard for money. I write books and create products that teach people how to have money work hard for them."
~ Robert Kiyosaki

REFERENCES

Ramsey Solutions (n.d.). Money ruining marriages in America. Business Wire. https://www.businesswire.com/news/home/20180207005698/en/Money- Ruining-Marriages-America

The State Science & Technology Institute (SSTI). (2023). Large percentage of Americans report they're struggling to make ends meet. *Author*. https://ssti.org/blog/large-percentage-americans-report-they%E2%80%99re-struggling-make-ends-meet#:~:text=Almost%2040%25%20of%20American%20adults,%25)%20and%20Arkansas%20(45.6%25).

U.S. News and World Report. (2022). Record number of Americans have bank accounts, gov't says. *Author*. https://www.usnews.com/news/business/articles/2022-10-25/record-number-of-americans-have-bank-accounts-govt-says

United States Court. (2023). Bankruptcy filings rise 13 percent. *Author*. https://www.uscourts.gov/news/2023/10/26/bankruptcy-filings-rise-13- percent

Weiss, B. (2022). Why financial literacy alone will always fail. *Personal Finance Kiplinger*. https://www.kiplinger.com/personal-finance/604578/why-financial-literacy-alone-will-always-fail

Urban, C. & Valdes, O. (2022). Why is measured financial literacy declining and what does it mean? maybe we just "Don't Know."

FINRA: Investor Education Foundation. https://finrafoundation.org/sites/finrafoundation/files/Why-Is-Measured-Financial-Literacy-Declining.pdf

Bureau of Economic Analysis. (2023). Personal income and

outlays, September 2023. *Author.*
https://www.bea.gov/news/2023/personal-income-and-outlays-september-2023

Capital One Shopping. (2023, June 11). How many Americans have credit cards? *Author.*
https://capitaloneshopping.com/research/how-many-americans-have-credit-cards/

Lending Club, (2022). 69% of Americans in Urban areas are living paycheck to paycheck; 14 percentage points higher than suburban consumers. *Author.*
https://ir.lendingclub.com/news/news-details/2023/69-of-Americans-in-Urban-Areas-are-Living-Paycheck-to-Paycheck-14-Percentage-Points-Higher-than-Suburban-Consumers/default.aspx

Lusardi, A. & Messay, F. (2023). The importance of financial literacy and its impact on financial wellbeing. *Cambridge University Press.* https://www.cambridge.org/core/journals/journal-of-financial-literacy-and-wellbeing/article/importance-of-financial-literacy-and-its-impact-on-financial-wellbeing/A5DBBF9D6F0696E5FD3733241EE28E66

BIBLE VERSES

The New American Standard Bible The New Living Trans

Marcella Joanne "MJ" Haskins Biography

Marcella Joanne "MJ" Haskins, in business known as MJ, is a native of New Castle, Delaware, the first state. MJ was born with an innate determination and optimism to persevere and succeed. She is most passionate about financial literacy and an advocate and supporter of financial education-to say the least. MJ has experienced both poverty and middle class living which gives her a unique insight when it comes to teaching, reaching and relating to people about personal finances.

MJ has more than 25 years of experience and knowledge in the Financial Services industry. She holds a Bachelor of Arts degree in Business Administration from the prestigious Bennett College for Women in Greensboro, North Carolina. She is proud to be a Delawarean and has always had an entrepreneurial spirit. As a result of her upbringing and education, she owns a Financial Consulting agency located in Middletown, Delaware. This is where she provides Individual & Small Business financial services including Tax & Estate Planning.

For 10 years, MJ volunteered for the Delaware Money Management Program; an agency that helped the elderly and disabled to pay their bills. The DMMP program is now called Stand By Me, which provides Delawareans with one-on-one coaching services to reach their money goals and provide peace of mind. The Stand By Me program is as a result of MJ planting a seed in the mind of the founder, Mary Dupont of Ted Talks.

SNAPSHOT OF MJ's SERVICE OFFERINGS

Individual Counseling & Coaching

MJ specializes in offering personal financial coaching to families and individuals, focusing on money and credit management, wealth building and protection. Services are provided to the clients based on their distinct financial needs, with an emphasis on educating clients with the following:

- Developing a spending plan

- Managing income & expenses, modifying spending & shopping behaviors

- Understanding, reading and restoring credit report and raising credit score

- Reducing and/or eliminating debt

- Fulfilling financial goals and large purchases (homeownership, vehicle or electric car, washer or dryer, home furnace or central air, roof, solar panels, vacation, holiday funds, wardrobes, etc.)

- Looking at ways to generate more income

- Learning about investment options (digital currency, stocks/mutual funds, bonds, CD's, and real estate)

- Ensuring assets are protected via estate planning

SEMINARS

MJ & Associates conduct customized seminars aimed at empowering individuals, affinity groups, employees of private and government agencies, religious entities (such as churches or mosques), community centers, libraries, civic organizations, group homes, shelters, meet-up groups, senior centers, hospital education and outreach plus followers on social media platforms such as Facebook, Fanbase, Instagram, LinkedIn, TikTok, YouTube, X and more.

MJ's seminars are tailored to suit the specific needs of each audience she serves. The goal is to share information that is easily retained and able to be applied almost immediately. MJ's seminars utilize understandable financial language that simplifies complex money and credit management concepts, making it easy for participants to grasp and interact with the discussion in a fun and colorful way!

For more products & services offered by MJ, please visit www.MJHaskins.com

CONTACT US

WE WOULD LOVE TO HEAR FROM YOU!

Send all correspondence to:
MJ Haskins
108 Patriot Drive
Middletown, Delaware
19709

Email us to book a seminar, speaking engagement, or to order more books and forward your questions, comments, or suggestions to:
covenantceo@gmail.com

www.MJHaskins.com